Light

Shadows, Mirrors, and Rainbows

T0052979

Written by Natalie M. Rosinsky
Illustrated by Sheree Boyd

Content Adviser: Dr. Paul Ohmann, Assistant Professor of Physics, University of St. Thomas, St. Paul, Minnesota
Reading Adviser: Lauren A. Liang, M.A., Literacy Education, University of Minnesota, Minneapolis, Minnesota

AMAZING SCIENCE

PICTURE WINDOW BOOKS
MINNEAPOLIS, MINNESOTA

Editor: Nadia Higgins
Designer: Melissa Voda
Page production: The Design Lab
The illustrations in this book were prepared digitally.

PICTURE WINDOW BOOKS
1710 Roe Crest Drive
North Mankato, MN 56003
www.capstonepub.com

Library of Congress Cataloging-in-Publication Data
Rosinsky, Natalie M. (Natalie Myra)
  Light : shadows, mirrors, and rainbows / written by Natalie M. Rosinsky ; illustrated by Sheree Boyd.
    v. cm. — (Amazing science) Includes bibliographical references and index.
    Contents: Delightful light—What makes shadows?—How do mirrors work?—What makes a rainbow?
  ISBN 978-1-4048-0013-7 (hardcover)
  ISBN 978-1-4048-0332-9 (paperback)
  1. Light—Juvenile literature. 2. Optics—Juvenile literature. [1. Light. 2. Optics.] I. Boyd, Sheree, ill. II. Title.
  QC360 .R67 2003
  535—dc21   2002005739

TABLE OF CONTENTS

Delightful Light

Shadows play on a sunny day. Water glints and gleams. At a storm's end, a rainbow bends.

Wherever you look, light dazzles and dances. It makes wonderful shapes and colors. Light is what lets you see things.

Fun fact: Light comes from the sun. Other natural light is made by lightning, fireflies, and the northern lights that shine in the Arctic.

Light comes from lightbulbs of all shapes, colors, and sizes.

Fun fact: Even when a room is dark, you can still see shapes and shadows. That means there must be a bit of light sneaking in.

Light streams out in rays. See the rays of light that stream from a movie projector in a dark theater. See the beam that travels from a flashlight.

What Makes Shadows?

When light rays are blocked, there are spots of darkness. The sun shines on you, but it can't shine through you.

Your body blocks the sunlight's path and makes a shadow that follows you wherever you go.

Sometimes your shadow is in front of you. Sometimes it's behind you. Can you guess why?

Even indoors, shadows jump across the walls and the floor.

Shine a flashlight at the wall. Then wiggle your fingers for some fun. Make shadow creatures that joke and jabber.

Inch your hand closer and closer to the flashlight. Your shadow creature gets bigger and bigger. What happens as you move your hand farther away from the flashlight?

How Do Mirrors Work?

When light hits something smooth and shiny, almost all of the light rays bounce, or reflect, off it.

When you see yourself in a mirror, light rays are bouncing from you to the mirror and back again. Your image is a reflection.

All around your house, reflections stare back at you. Look at your face in a silver toaster or a shiny spoon. These reflections look different from the one in a mirror.

The moon has no light of its own. Moonlight is really sunlight reflecting off the moon. At night, this reflection lights your path and paints the trees silver.

Fun fact: Not everything makes a shadow or a reflection. Light can go right through objects that are clear. Moonlight can stream through a window, making a bright spot on the floor.

What Makes a Rainbow?

A ray of sunlight is like a rope that's made of many strands. Each strand has its own color—red, orange, yellow, green, blue, or violet (purple).

After a storm, the air is often filled with water droplets. When rays of sunlight shine through the droplets, the rays fray like rope. All the colors in the rays separate and bend in slightly different directions.

Fun fact: On a sunny day, you might see a rainbow in the spray of a garden hose. You can see rainbow colors in a diamond's sparkle or on a delicate soap bubble.

17

A rainbow arches across the sky. Look up and see the parade of colors that are wrapped inside every single ray of sunlight.

You can't see all the colors that are in a rainbow. The colors of light at the far ends of a rainbow are invisible to people. These colors are infrared light and ultraviolet light.

Not-so-fun fact: Ultraviolet light from the sun can burn your skin.

All around, light is sparkling, swirling, blinking, bending, and bouncing.

Watch. Wonder. Investigate. Our world is shining with colorful new things to explore.

Out-of-Sight Experiments

Make a Loony Spoon Mirror: Get a large, shiny metal spoon. Hold it up in front of your face, with the inside of the spoon curving toward you. How is your reflection on the spoon different from your reflection in a mirror? Now, turn the spoon around and look at your reflection on the back of the spoon. How does this change your reflection? Fun-house mirrors play with reflections in this way.

Make Your Own Rainbow: Fill a bowl with water and put it in front of a sunny window. Place a mirror in the bowl, with its shiny side facing the sunlight. Lean the mirror against one side of the bowl so it is standing up. (If it won't stand up by itself, you can just hold it with your hands.) Now have a friend hold a piece of white paper outside the bowl, across from the mirror.

The water in the bowl will separate the sunlight into colors and the mirror will reflect it. A small rainbow will spread out on the white paper. You may need to tilt the mirror a bit to really get an eyeful of color.

Shadow Tag: Here's another way to play tag with a group of friends on a sunny day. Choose one person to be "it." Everyone else makes a big circle around her. When she says "go," you run! Don't let her stomp on your shadow! Look at all the ways you can move your body to keep your shadow safe. If you get caught, you're the next shadow stomper. The person you catch will be the stomper after that. The person who can go the longest without getting caught is the winner.

Enlightening Facts

Bright and Hot: Light is energy and can heat things up. Sunlight can warm your neck and shoulders. It can make a sidewalk so hot that it burns your bare feet. Things that block light take in the light's heat.

Life-Giving Light: Plants use sunlight to make food so they can grow tall. As plants grow, they give off the oxygen that we need to breathe. If there were no light, Earth would be too cold for anything to live on it. There would be no plants, no food, and no oxygen.

Faster than Fast: Light is the fastest moving thing in the whole universe. In air, light rays travel at about 186,000 miles per second. That's 10 million times as fast as a car on the highway.

Starry Light: Scientists learn about stars by studying a star's light. Starlight tells us how fast a star is moving, and whether it's moving away from Earth or toward it. The colors that make up the light from a star can even tell scientists what the star is made of.

Trick Legs: Look down at your legs when you stand in a swimming pool. They look stubby and short. That's because light bends as it goes from the air to the water. The bent light makes your legs look shorter than they really are.

Glossary

infrared—one of the colors of the rainbow that we can't see. It is next to red in the rainbow.

rainbow—an arc of the separate colors that make up sunlight

ray—a line of light that beams out from something bright

reflect—to bounce off an object. Smooth, shiny objects like a mirror or water reflect a lot of light.

reflection—the image that forms when light has bounced off a shiny object

shadow—the dark shape made when something blocks light

ultraviolet—one of the colors of the rainbow that we can't see. It comes after violet in the rainbow.

violet—another word for purple

To Learn More

At the Library

Branley, Franklyn Mansfield. Day Light, Night Light: Where Light Comes From. New York: HarperCollins, 1998.

Gold-Dworkin, Heidi. Exploring Light and Color. New York: McGraw-Hill, 2000.

Graham, Joan Bransfield. Flicker Flash: Poems. Boston: Houghton Mifflin, 1999.

Fact Hound

Fact Hound offers a safe, fun way to find Web sites related to this book. All of the sites on Fact Hound have been researched by our staff.
http://www.facthound.com

1. Visit the Fact Hound home page.
2. Enter a search word related to this book, or type in this special code: 1404800131.
3. Click the FETCH IT button.

Your trusty Fact Hound will fetch the best sites for you!

Index